Doodleology

Andy Cannon

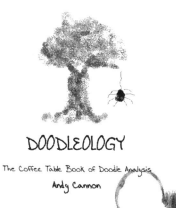

DOODLEOLOGY

The Coffee Table Book of Doodle Analysis

Andy Cannon

Doodleology

3rd Edition Copyright © 2013 Andy Cannon – All Rights Reserved

ISBN: 978-1-291-55316-1

Contents

Introduction

Of Doodles, the Mind, Logic and Symbolism

Hello,

I'm genuinely glad you've decided to pick this book up, and that you share my passion for getting inside someone's head and working out what makes us tick. And doodles and drawings are one of the many ways I do this – by learning to analyze people's drawings and doodles and to be able to tell people, finally, what their drawing says about them. That is the premise and purpose of this little book.

Where to begin...

Doodles are seemingly so incredibly abstract – I kind of compare them to dreaming, because they take on a mind of their own and seemingly merge, twist and transform seamlessly. You may start out by writing a name and with spiraling twisting strokes it blossoms into a forest and then a waterfall. You know, you could be writing down numbers while on the phone, or in a meeting and a few minutes later your look down and as if from nowhere a desert island has emerged on your sheet of paper surrounded by flying boxes or some kind of space ship, or what looks like a complex maze...like dreams, they form without really making sense to you.

And like dreams, doodles are a conduit or channel for our right brain*, our inner and more mystical processes. A channel for the subconscious mind.

So how can we become an expert on them? ... Well we can't. Much like with dreams, we are not really in a position of authority to tell people what their dreams or doodles mean; the only person who truly has that authority is the dreamer or the doodler. But we can make some pretty good guesses and even involve the doodler to help us analyze and interpret them.

We will do this by using a little symbolism, logic and intuition.

Symbolism, according to Wikipedia: *is the applied use of symbols. It is a representation that carries a particular meaning. It is a device in literature where an object represents an idea. A **symbol** is an object, action, or idea that represents something other than itself.*

If I may follow on from Wikipedia and say that a symbol often represents something more profound, for instance the horse can represent a messenger and the delivery of urgent information. The sun can represent warmth, creativity, life and the child in all of us.

Our mind works with images and metaphors; it finds patterns and decodes meaning. And often the way we see and interpret signs, images or symbols is determined by our culture and our life experiences.

Carl Jung, a famous Psychologist and father of Jungian Psychology was, I believe, one of the first to put forward the idea of the Collective Unconscious, sometimes referred to as the Collective Subconscious. The essence of which is that we have a hidden pool or reservoir of wealth and experiences to tap into which we have inherited through generations and which we, in turn, will add to. It has also been suggested that this hidden reservoir of knowledge is in fact formed of a body of energy that we have the power to tap into. Evidence of which is in our understanding of archetypes (the Shadow, the Self.., or perhaps Greek and Roman Archetypes, gods and mythologies as well) to put it simply.

Jung and later Arrien Angeles, in her book 'Signs of Life', proposed an example: throughout the world people draw certain things; suns, moons, stars and trees in a similar way. Five signs in particular are universally recognized and assigned a meaning – these being: Circle, Square, Cross, Triangle and Spiral (which is one of the oldest). The Triangle for instance, was associated with goals, ambitions, hopes and dreams and was seen as a power symbol; people who favour this symbol are seen to have certain traits which we will see later.

Logic and Deduction: In essence there might be a clear, definable reason for a person's doodle or drawing. For instance: It may be a sketch of something in front of them or present in the room. It may be directly related to their current state of mind; known as mood congruent theory. Another example would be, a person who is angry is more likely to apply firmer pressure on the pen and leave a dark, thicker line – logic or deduction would suggest that at the time of drawing or doodling this person was angry or even excited.

Intuition: Is allowing our right-brains to see, sense and feel and allow interpretations and meanings to flow and come to us.

That all sounds quite a lot to take in and a little complicated, but in truth once you enable your right brain to view and analyze drawings intuitively and begin applying your own level of natural knowing alongside some minor left-brain work of logic and deduction, you'll find with a little practice that you'll become quite adept. I hope the information to follow will help you on your journey of doodle analysis. You'll find this to be a GREAT ice-breaker, entertaining piece for a party and even something to make or raise money from.

Good luck and when we meet I'll be excited to have *you* analyze my doodle.

Andy Cannon, Barcelona, 2012

www.andycannon.com

P.S. Some of the doodle reading techniques in this book have their place in genuine projective psychological tests. I've steered away from dwelling on the stronger and darker psychological tests and drawing analysis theories because the world is a dark enough place and I like to use this ability, this skill, this game, to focus on the more positive qualities and to have fun and entertain rather than attempt to diagnose.

* See the further on for a mini-article about the right and left sides of the brain.

The Flow

Before I talk about The Flow of a reading, let's look at some of the ways we may begin the reading.

a) – From the notebooks or pieces of paper left by the doodler, or the secretary at the Doctor's.

b) – From a purposefully drawn doodle. I often get people to draw or doodle something on a large index card or in the pages of my Doodle Journal. In this case we must realize that this isn't strictly a doodle. As doodles are generally drawn or scribbled without much conscious thought while someone is preoccupied with the likes of a phone call, business meeting or when they are day dreaming. Whereas a drawing is often drawn with conscious thought.

We can, however, apply many of the elements and techniques of doodle analysis to people's drawings. This next section looks at some of these techniques and also includes a doodle dictionary, so to speak. Use the dictionary and these symbolic interpretations as a guide for your own natural intuition and knowing. Collect your drawings or doodles and analyze them with the help of this book and these sections to really help this become second nature.

Our reading will progress much easier once we have established a path to follow. From this path we may deviate or explore other trails; following them and returning back to our original path when one trail comes to an end. My Flow continually changes and adapts and yours will too, but working with this structure will be of great help to you.

1 – Look at the back of the drawing and discuss the importance of pressure and what their pressure means.

2 – Look at the front and give your initial impressions based on positions, lines and your initial intuitive right-brain feelings.

3 – Then discuss what they drew. Do some of the traits of their drawing support the previous discussion or contradict them? Here I will throw a little example of them:

"...you're someone who just cannot let go of anything – I imagine you keep dead batteries, pieces of wire and random pen-tops because 'maybe they'll come in handy' , you're hoarder and just cannot throw anything..."

4 – Deduce and discuss possible strengths and weaknesses.

5 – Additional impressions or 'advice' on using their strengths or overcoming their weaknesses.

If you wish you can turn to the examples page now to look at a sample doodle and how I've applied The Flow.

The Doodle's position on the Page

Let's take a look at what the location of the doodle on the page can tell us.

TOP: Independent, Spiritual, Up in the air, Enthusiastic

CORNERS: Suggests someone shy or timid

RIGHT: Urge to express oneself or reveal hidden thoughts

CENTRE: Organized, Extrovert, Need for space

LEFT: Held or drawn to the past, Sensitive, Fear of exposure

If a drawing/doodle is centre left, then use a combination of the centre and left readings. Top and right, then a mix of top and right readings... and so on and so forth.

BOTTOM: Critical, Practical, Reliable, At times depressive

Pressure

By looking at pressure; how much force the artist has applied to the pen or pencil when drawing we can come to few conclusions

HEAVY PRESSURE – Indicates strength, natural energy and drive. May not be modest. Often a sign of a manual labourer or passionate and creative person. Also can symbolise depression.

MEDIUM PRESSURE – Generally well-balanced, confident, a happy medium between HEAVY and LIGHT.

LIGHT PRESSURE – A sign of a sensitive, spiritual and idealistic person. Introverted and critical. Perhaps lacking in drive and libido. A desire to be inconspicuous.

VARYING PRESSURES – Light pressure with bursts of heavy pressure may suggest a person lacking patience and prone to outbursts of temper. Constantly changing pressure could suggest the person is going through a state of change or is perhaps imbalanced or unstable.

Lines and Curves

Doodleology is about getting into the mindset of the doodler. Asking why would I draw that, and why would I draw it LIKE that? One of the easiest places in which to see this, is in looking at the lines, curves and pressure applied to the paper.

If the lines are frenzied, sharp and jagged with sharp protrusions and multiple edges with few curvy lines then the doodler's mindset is reflected by the nature of the lines...aggressive, angry and defensive...perhaps the doodle was drawn during an argument.

On the other hand you may see more thoughtful spirals and curls as the doodler is calmer and their hand is flowing across the paper with fewer cares.

Traditional graphology would tell us that numerous circular strokes indicate a dependency on others, someone not particularly assertive and perhaps a sign of effeminacy. Definitely not always the case, judge it by how you feel when you retrace or copy their doodles and lines. Traditionally, rhythmic and fluid strokes are drawn by people hoping to escape from reality, or maybe they are daydreaming right now.

The Doodle's Content

Doodles come in all shapes and sizes – dollar signs and boxes, to complex mini murals sprawling and morphing like a city across the page of a book. We'll begin by looking at the basic make up – simple shapes and designs. Among the most common are basic 3D objects, arrows and simple shapes. There are interesting universal associations with the following shapes and it'll pay to remember them as you begin your journey into doodle analysis, as the role these shapes play may be as important as the drawing itself.

CIRCLES – By itself the circle can talk about independence and seeking your own space to grow and develop or in groups of little circles hinting at parts of you that seem separate or distant from each other. In a more developed flowing doodle, such as the centre of a flower, I see it also representing your social circle, the people you gather around you, and its size and the flamboyance of its surroundings, a mirror of yours.

SQUARES – Is someone who is all about home and family. These are key values in this person's life. It is also about strength about stability and the desire to reinforce stability and to protect their home. Stacking together these boxes is you juggling together all these pieces, family, friends and money, trying to make everything that bit more stable. Organised neat boxes could come from someone particularly meticulous and who can be quite controlling at times.

TRIANGLE – Power and ambition – this is a powerful symbol and shows drive and determination. Someone who may stop at nothing to get somewhere and achieve a lot, but may feel short in other areas of life and leave behind family and friends to pursue, at times a mis-guided direction.

One only has to look to the pyramids, the mountains to understand these are about your goals, ambitions, dreams and visions. They also appear as arrows, and at times staircases. In doodles, the arrow is normally drawn sharply and numerously depending on the person's goal or desire at the time. A person doodling the triangles has goals and ambitions and really wants to make a change. They fear not having ambitions. Do they have many different ambitions and goals represented in different triangular forms?

SPIRALS – Drawn by a person who doesn't want to be pinned in and/or be normal. Showing a different side of themselves and living and thinking outside the box are key traits of their personality.

Whether as a classic whirlpool-like spiral or twisting spiralling lines, they are doodled by people who thrive on variety, creativity, growth and change. The person will often and easily get drawn into many different subjects and interests at once, starting up new projects but not always following through. Being someone who is very drawn to the spiral in life and doodling, I can tell you we appreciate our multiple interests and achievements being acknowledged, but need space and flexibility in our relationships.

CROSSES – The cross is a sign of relationships and dependency. Whether on friends/lovers/God/god/gods or goddesses. Are relationships in the mind of the doodler at this time? What are they leaning on or finding support and dependency in?

The cross is seen as two parts creating a whole, and Plato talks of creature who joins broken parts of the world's soul with a cross. I remember reading one doodle with the doodler, where two trees crossed, finding support with one another. We saw it as the perfect metaphor for her relationship with her brother, one of mutual support and dependence on each other.

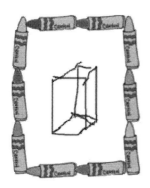

3D OBJECTS or Doodles with a 3D ELEMENT

Are indicative of clever thinkers who can see the big picture and other people's perspectives. Boxes are often drawn because this is the first step learnt in technical drawing. Stacked boxes (3D or otherwise) may suggest someone who is under stress. Some doodles will have a 3D element or seem to have a particular geometric shape in them (or perhaps something like an arrow/ladder) – e.g. triangles as cat's ears for example. When this happens, you can mention that this – e.g. with a 3D house, boat etc...suggests to me that you often strive to see things from every perspective and try to get an understanding of the whole event as it happens – I'd imagine that when you find something that interests you, you enjoy researching it from various different angles.

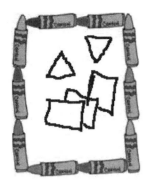

GEOMETRIC SHAPES

Specifically squares and triangles in regular patterns suggests someone organised and logical. An efficient person with good planning skills and a sense of purpose. Triangles – a desire to improve one's status – remember ambition. Power. Drive

ARROWS, LADDERS & STAIRS

Ambitious, wants to achieve and be successful and probably has some big goals ahead. You should consider the direction and size of the arrow e.g. straight up suggests a desire to get to the top. Many arrows in different directions may suggest someone who has too many options. Aggressively drawn arrows hint at a desire to take action.

SUNS, MOONS, STARS, ASTRAL BODIES

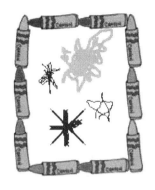

Optimistic, enthusiastic, ambitious. A person keen for others to take notice of them.

A sun hints at a more childlike and happy disposition. These come in many different forms. I've had suns made up of spiral patterns with triangles representing the rays, to starry skies (the number of stars could turn out to be significant), so ask questions and check out the mini-article about colours and numbers later on in the book. The sun's rays to me, indicates a desire to stretch out and make connections, a symbol of how someone likes to reach out – with the triangles for rays it was about how they often like to show off ambition and determination to let people know they are good and have a talent at something, but at times they must be aware that people may take this as 'bragging' and that they would benefit more from making social connections than always striving for business connections.

The moon has strong ties with the feminine and mystical. Is it a curved moon facing Right? Then this means exploring new creative potentional. Or facing left – suggesting that now is a time to clear away the thoughts of the past and begin with something new.

FOOD

Drawn by people who like food. Perhaps they are or have been on a diet. They might also have other issues, cravings or medical concerns that is bringing food to the forefront of their mind. Could the person be a cook or a baker, and the drawing is of something they are particularly good at? An ice-cream – what favour is it?

I had this case once with a baker who made delicious cup-cakes. But the topic earlier had also been about cup-cakes, which leads us to a point; often if you are talking or joking about something beforehand in a casual manner, when the person is put on the spot to draw something, they will draw what you were just talking about – perhaps as kind of in-joke or just because they couldn't think of anything else at that time.

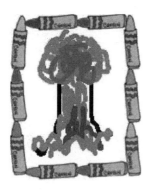

TREES

Much like the house they are open to many interpretations that are covered more indepth a few chapters on.

HEARTS

A romantic. Someone in love, doodling with someone special in mind. Normally strong interpersonal relationships are on the mind when your see heart doodles. I remember one particularly telling doodle drawn by a student of mine; several hearts were scattered around the page, then towards the lower righthand side was a pair of lips with arrows pointing to them from all directions. Definitely romance and love on the mind.

A cracked heart – more a sign of a break-up or miscommunication, with loved ones on the mind.

CARS, BOATS, PLANES, TRAINS

The doodler has a desire to travel. Perhaps to get away from something or their current circumstances. Particularly luxurious cars hint at a strong materialistic side. Later on I discuss how to read animals and how the direction the animal is facing factors into the interpretation. To the right means looking forward and looking to the future, and facing to the left means looking back on the past. Guess what? You can apply these to drawings of cars and the like as well! I very rarely get cars or planes, I seem to get boats and trains more often. Again, try to identify certain factors; does the boat have an anchor weighing it down or keeping it moored – a person wanting to escape but perhaps kept from escaping – is the boat facing stormy seas?

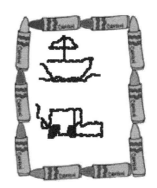

HOUSES

An indicator of how secure someone feels. Houses are associated with family life. Does the house look welcoming or foreboding? You can play with your interpretation a lot here as well as take some ideas from a projective psychology test called the House-Person-Tree Test (which is beyond the scope of this book). How welcoming does the house look? How many windows does it have? How big are the windows? Particularly big windows and bathroom windows are said to be indicative of an exhibitionist side to the person. Does it have a fence? This could mean that they are a little protective and like to keep people at a distance before letting them into their lives. A path? A sign that someone is open to communication. Is there smoke coming from the chimney? Is it a house or an apartment block? Are there any flowers or trees? Is it in a row of houses or just one house? A row of houses suggests the person doesn't want to be alone or prefers to follow rather than to lead. Sometimes, if I cannot or do not know what a particular feature of the drawing looks like, I point it out and ask them what it means e.g. – "Interesting, I see (you've drawn a moat around your house) – why did you do this and what does this mean to you?" You don't have to have all the answers. Let them tell you what they think something means and work and read from that. (FYI – Think of anything like a moat or a fence as being a boundary – a layer of protection if you will to prevent their real self or personality being shown, or from people getting close too them.)

WEBS

Feeling trapped or a wish to entrap someone. Possibly drawn by a Goth or someone interested in the spooky or bizarre. A web WITHOUT links hints at a systematic and analytical person.

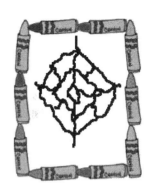

SYMBOLS

You will from time to time get symbols and even corporate logos drawn. The Ying Yang and the peace symbol are a common occurrence in this area. Sometimes these come out of the blue and not from a person you would have expected them from. For some reason, creating a reading around these is quite hard – one reason is because the intrinsic nature of these types of symbols means you cannot use some of the material from the Lines and Curves chapter. Could the symbols indicate a love of something, for instance a superman logo could lead to the line: You're probably the kind of person who collects things – a collector – probably of comic books or perhaps action figures.

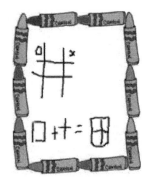

GAMES & PICTURE PUZZLES

The drawings of a logical and competitive person. What style of game is being played? Chess boards could indicate problems to be solved or moves and solutions the person may be looking for.

ANIMALS

A protective person, warm, sensitive and considerate. The desire to defend. Could perhaps just love animals. Drawings of bugs, spiders and mice may indicate a phobia. In shamanic traditions, spiders, especially bearing fangs are a sign of energetic or spiritual intrusions. And large animals (elephants, lions) a desire to feel more masculine. It's really important to think of all the factors and possibilities of the purpose behind a drawing. Native American symbolism sees horses as being messengers. They are majestic creatures.

Once a girl drew a penguin. Why? She was going to the zoo in a few days' time and was particularly excited about seeing the penguins. What can this piece of information tell us and what can we then tell her about herself?

Butterflies are interesting as they can be interpreted like a flower: suggesting a delicate side and love of nature's intricacies, and also a sign that someone could be a 'social butterfly'. You can also suggest it shows a sign of an interest in reincarnation or perhaps their soul's search for reincarnation (depending on their character) or even perhaps their desire to change and spread their wings and fly away. I haven't had a drawing of a caterpillar yet – but that would be interesting.

Birds - Will perhaps, one day, be the subject of a more in depth discussion. We see them often drawn by people who also draw ferns and leaves - someone with a fondness for the beauty and intricacies in nature. Further symbolism of the bird talks about communication and the desire to communicate with someone far away. Perhaps the bird doodled is perched and indicates someone being particular watchful or careful. Maybe a flock of birds is heading away from the future, a bad sign ... or towards the future a better omen for their outlook.

FISH

Fish and underwater creatures often represent someone going with the flow and someone who may find themselves going between various different emotional states fairly quickly. They are tackling new elements and becoming ready for new beginnings.

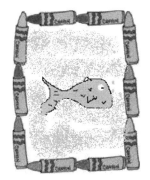

Fish are generally drawn by people who are going through a period of study or intensive research. Perhaps the person is in university or has recently taken to researching a new subject or a particular course. With my doodlers, I've found that a right facing fish is often inspired to study by a goal or ambition they have in mind. A left facing fish is studying as the result of something that has inspired and stimulated them in the past and that they want to keep present and important in their lives.

The more obvious the presence of water the stronger the emotional link to their studies, or current place in the world.

FACES & FACIAL FEATURES

A good looking face suggests the person is positive and loves people. They are good natured, humane and social. A person who is very talkative will often draw an open mouth on the face. An ugly face shows a dislike or distrust of people. They lack self-confidence, get defensive and are perhaps bad tempered and aggressive.

Faces vary a lot between a simple circle with two dots and a smile to fully fledged mini portraits. The only little tip I can share is to look for the style of a face, as this may hint at some of the person's influences. E.g., Recently I've had a couple of faces which looked clearly Manga-esque. I've had vaguely Simpson-esque characters and often cartoony faces sticking out their tongues – which I've interpreted as a sign of a mischievousness and slightly cocky side. The hair can be used too – a spiky doo or long very wavy hair is someone who wants to be seen as being a cool, chilled and fun person to be around. A tighter shorter hairstyle is indicative of a more reserved personality.

Lips – Suggest a sexual desire.

Eyes – Eyes can represent a number of things. Many eyes or pairs of eyes seem to suggest a paranoia of being watched. Interestingly one particularly watchful and artistic eye represents both the more introspective side of you and your love of finding the beauty in things. They also represent the unknown, a window to the soul, beauty and mystery. Often times the doodler will have this sense of being always watched and will have a strong interest in the natural beauty and mystery behind the eye – these two traits seem to come together more often than not.

Consider whether the eye may represent their personality (big and open, narrow and closed). Recently, I'm seeing in younger people a tendency to draw Manga type eyes. And how we doodle or sketch cartoony characters and figures hints at our influences and what we watch and choose to imitate.

A lot of these things you can play with yourself – it may not come to you right away but if you keep their drawing and look over it again later you'll suddenly release the connection that was there to be made, but seemed to escape you at the time.

LANDSCAPES: BEACHES, MOUNTAINS...

Often point to someone who wants to get away from life at that moment. Maybe where they want to go or where they want to escape to. A dream location?

There is normally a lot to work with here. If there are birds in the picture, use those in the reading. If there is a tree, incorporate a tree reading. A boat? A beach towel – is there one or two? A sandcastle...all these little things can add a lot to the reading. Sometimes just pointing them out is interesting. How does the sea look – choppy or calm? This could symbolise the person's troubles or how they feel about the future or the present. The same with clouds, these could represent problems or worries looming.

How about a snowy mountain with skiers; we can see the doodler's likes and sometimes their dislikes – a mountain with a little bear lurking...which is beautiful and fun to enjoy, but a sense of wild unknown danger...are they a little like that?

FLOWERS

Flowers are generally drawn by women, to the extent it kind of sticks in your head when a man draws them. I read these doodlers as potential romantics, a person to whom lasting friendships and social relations is important. These are covered in a lot more detail, along with trees, a few pages later on.

DRINKS

This is a particularly socially spirited sign. I have two observations about drinks. Wine glasses and beer bottles I have encountered in social drinking and party situations. Coffee cups I have had doodled several times – in fact at least twice from Argentinian girls. In Argentina the drinking of Maté (not coffee but a green tea sipped through an ornate straw), is culturally very important – a sign of friendship.

WATER – RIVERS, STREAMS, SEAS

Water has been long understood as an expression of the state of the subconscious and therefore the doodler's emotional state. A boat on water is the desire to travel and escape from the emotions and situations they are currently finding themselves in.

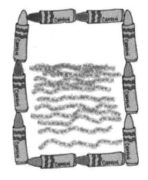

A stormy sea or rough river is a telltale sign that life at the moment is pretty rough and their emotions are being tossed around and taking them in different directions.

Does the water appear by their house, or a large tranquil lagoon beneath a mountain, or a stream passing a tree? This can be another insight into their current emotions.

MONSTERS

Whether literal or a person or face with strong disfiguarations or monster-like traits, I consider these as being a personification of an inner struggle, or the representation of inner dilemmas or wounds that need healing.

DIRTY DOODLES

Boobies and Willies! Let's face it – you know someone's gonna draw them. You can have a lot of fun with it.

Additional Details

Proportions

Does everything on the paper looked organised and in place? Well, that's what it says about the artiste. They are organised and like things to be in good order, perhaps even obsessively so.

Details

Have they included loads of little details? Well, then you can say:

"this person has a marvelous attention to detail" – then perhaps tie it in with something you can see about them – "I'd imagine your home is very coloured co-ordinated."

Speed

Did they rush the drawing or take their time? Someone with a lack of patience may very well rush their drawings. Someone who takes their time, probably does so in life as well and has a lot more patience.

Relationship

Look at the individual elements of the drawing and the relationship they each share. For example, what if someone draws a tree and a person hiding behind the tree. Your tree reading now takes a different path. Maybe you have a house and there are flowers around the house. Why not combine them into one reading? Maybe you could read the house as representing the subject, and the flowers as friends or siblings. Are the flowers close to the house or far away – this could reveal how emotionally close they feel to those friends or family members.

Is it Finished ?

Has the person finished the drawing? Or perhaps the lines don't really meet where they should e.g. if you draw a square but the four lines do not touch one another. This suggests they may often leave things incomplete or unfinished and often find themselves rushing to complete things at the last moment.

External Factors

Throughout I have mentioned that there are external factors as well as internal factors to consider. This means that the drawing could be influenced by something you were just talking about.

The doodle could also be a result of a person's hobby or interests, like the baker who drew cupcakes. It could be as simple as something they can see behind you or on the table, like perhaps a wine or cocktail glass. Perhaps they have just bought a new house or a new ladder! Or maybe they are just really psyched about going on a sailing trip tomorrow. But whether there are internal or external factors you will always have something to say, and if necessary find a way to give an internal reading.

E.G. If someone draws a cupcake!

"This looks like a fairly personal drawing. You see I get pictures of houses, dogs and trees – but a cupcake...this says something a bit more about you? Are you a baker? – ah ha! The fact you've drawn this suggests to me you're particularly proud of this fact and if

only a hobby now, it could be a career you're planning on going down...is that correct? I see you've drawn icing here – ok – don't think about this but just go with the first thing that comes into your head – if you were to colour your drawing in mentally what colour would the icing be?...Green? Interesting, any reason you chose that colour? No!? It just kind of popped into your head."

 *Now we can give a reading on the colour green (see the mini-article on colours towards the end of this book).

Tree Readings

__Before reading on, grab a pen and paper and take 3 minutes to draw or doodle a tree. Then analyze your own tree as you read along.__

The tree is seen as an individual's expression of how they see themselves and their life. It is their tree of life and tells the story of their life in a skeletal form. We can use them to help build rapport in social and business situations and also help people begin to open up and discuss their life situations, be they present or past.

Begin by noting the pressure and position of the tree.

Tree Types

There are several styles of tree a person may draw. Here are the main styles and their interpretations.

The Cotton Ball Tree

Drawn generally by happy and optimistic people. It has a very fluffy top. People who draw this are normally in a good place.

The Palm Tree

Drawn by someone who loves the little sensations and pleasures in life. They would also like to be by the beach or somewhere far away right now.

The Christmas Tree

Drawn by people who have a special affection for celebration and holidays.

The Winter Tree

Drawn by someone who is open and honest. They have nothing to hide. They would be good people to seek a truthful answer or opinion from.

The tree from the ground up is the representation of your life from birth (the base), through your past (the trunk) to where you are now (the foliage).

Base and Ground

These represent your early upbringing. A thick base that is wider than the trunk shows someone who had a good childhood and received a lot of support in their early years. A tree with no roots, no ground and no extra width suggests a distancing of themselves from their past.

The Trunk

The trunk below the foliage represents someone's past. The length of the trunk shows how long or hard it has been for them to get where they are now. A wide sturdy trunk shows someone strong-willed. A distortion of the trunk, such as through heavy shading suggests a particularly troublesome or difficult past. Knot holes in the trunk suggests a time in their life that was particularly traumatic and life-changing, something they may not yet have recovered from. At the top of the trunk where it meets the foliage, any forks in the trunk show a person who is trying to follow many paths and hasn't really made up their mind as to which path in life to follow.

Treetop

The treetop should be looked at in relation to the size of the tree trunk. If they are equal it shows a well-balanced person.

Details

Again pay attention to the tree and how it's drawn, as many things are self-explanatory. A particularly detailed and symmetrical tree suggests a very meticulous and organised person.

The presence of clouds could be a sign of problems or worries, and take a look at the position of the clouds, sun and birds – are they on the left (the past) or on the right (the present or future).

Birds, animals and people show the warm-hearted, nurturing side of the person – especially if they are sheltering or living in a tree.

Fruits and nuts could simply be just decoration for the tree or an appreciation of the extra comforts in life and an indicator of an ambitious desire they are working to bring into fruition.

In some cases, it can signify worries about fertility or a desire to start a family.

Grass and flowers growing beneath the tree are like an invitiation to invite friends and family under the doodler's wing and to be comfortable and happy around them.

Remember relationship of water to your emotions and feels, well, is there water present in the drawing – a small stream perhaps?

NOTE: I would favour doing tree readings if I was going to be giving readings to large groups of people, more so if they were private readings. Give them a nice sheet of A4, a pencil and an eraser and give them a good few minutes alone or away from the group to make their drawing.

You can then talk at length about their tree, and in doing so mark neatly in alternating colours interesting areas of the tree that draw your attention.

Flower Readings

The drawing of a flower is literally blooming with cues for a great reading. In many ways it's like a tree – and a great way to present flower and tree readings are as **"His & Her"**, the fella draws the tree and the chica doodles the flower.

In principle a doodle of a flower, tells us the doodler is likely, though not necessarily, female. Looking at the type of flower and the pressure, it is often foudn that many times a flower is from those with a gentle heart especially towards people and nature. Social relationships are important to the person – they often blossom in social situations – does the inner circle of the flower reflect this? Among men it could also be the sign of a potential romantic! Moreover they are a sign that something the person is doing in life is coming together and making sense.

The Appearance of the Doodle:

Is it wilting? Exotic!? Broken?! – What can these additional details tell us?

For example: A wilting flower could show that the person is feeling depressed or lacking something they need drastically – love, social support…they are responding in much the same way a flower might do when it is lacking water, sunlight, good soil etc. Is it wilting towards the left hand side, which would hint at something from the past affecting the present?

Leaves or How Many Flowers

I can give you two very interesting observations here – the number of leaves a flower or doodle has, is often linked to how many siblings or children the doodler has!!! The same goes for a bunch of flowers; the number of flowers often correlates with the doodler's family size.

The Base and Roots

A flower whose stem has no plant pot or some kind of base often shows a person who is or can easily detached themselves from the past – and compartmentalize themselves.

A base or ground shows someone who is supported or feels supported either now, or in their early life.

A plant pot shows someone who perhaps feels isolated at that moment or has led a rather isolated life, or is happy standing strong and by themselves. (To determine which you would have to look at other factors behind the drawing...pressure and location specifically.)

Don't forget the head of the flower or petals – again linked to family and friends and how close they are to them, and it could also show how happy this person is at the moment.

The Pig Test and other Animals

***Before reading on, grab a pen and paper and take a minute or two to doodle a pig.
Then analyze your pig as you read along.***

A well-known personality test. It's a great ice-breaker and great for walk-arounds or parties. People love it and love to learn it. I also use aspects of this when analysing drawings of animals other than pigs. I actually first encountered this about 10 years ago while on a first date with an art student – however she could only remember what the tail meant :) Feel free to use Doodleology in your dating life :)

OK, now take a look at your pig or your subject's pig as you go through this information. This pig trait information can be applied to other doodles or animals you encounter along the way.

Location of the Pig on the Page

I combine the details mentioned in pressure and position (previously) along with this.

Top: Someone with many hopes and dreams – very optimistic and positive.

Middle: Someone who is a realist and generally well-balanced. Often takes action as the voice of common sense.

Bottom: A little bit critical and pessimistic. Will probably be quite skeptical of the accuracy of their reading.

Direction the Pig is Facing

Facing left: Friendly and fairly traditional in their family life. Also could be good at handling numbers or dates. Much like with regards to the position on the page, the pig is looking back on the past and contemplating the past.

Facing right: An active person, often very independent from family life. Bad with remembering dates or dealing with numbers. Future orientated and ready to move forward.

Facing front: They may speak their mind, sometimes too often, as they are direct and do not fear discussion. They often play the role of Devil's Advocate.

Number of Visible Legs

4 legs: Secure and stubborn. Sticks to their ideals.

Less than 4: Going through a period of a change and are perhaps a little insecure.

More than 4!: Doesn't pay attention to details or has an over-active imagination.

Ears

Show how good a listener you are. The bigger the ears, the better at listening. No ears – you need to start listening to other people.

Mouth

Big Mouth: Opinionated and likes to give advice. Considers themselves to be the life of the party.

Smile: A sunny deposition and looks on the bright side of things.

No Mouth: Generally a quiet person. My need to put more faith in themselves when they speak their mind.

Details

A detailed pig hints at an analytical, cautious and or distrustful person.

Little or no detail are signs of a risk-taker and someone that is perhaps emotional and naive.

Tail

Guaranteed to raise a smile when you tell them what this means. The longer the length of the tail the better your love life/higher your sex drive. In other animals this is often seen in other well known or particularly important features of that animal, for instance in the length of the tusks of an elephant.

Doodleology In Action

Now we've gathered a little more insight into the psychology behind doodles, we are going to try our hand at analysing them. I have included a few sample doodles here, and a few quick interpretations of my own. See if you can make your own interpretation before reading mine.

I suggest you first say it out loud as you refer back to pages in this book, and then write it down in a more concise form, adding additional details you notice as you go.

Example 1 :: Coconuts and Surf!!!

Pressure: Medium – Heavy *(CREATIVE – WELL-BALANCED)*.

Lines: Fluid and rhythmic *(ESCAPE FROM REALITY)*.

Position: Whole paper *(ORGANISED, EXTROVERT)*.

Picture: Beach Landscape *(ESCAPE FROM REALITY, EXOTIC, TRAVEL)*, coconut tree *(EXOTIC/RELAXING)*, sea, sand, sun – low in sky, drawn without rays perhaps a sunrise or sunset *(IDEALIST, ROMANTIC)*. Detailed and well proportioned *(INTELLIGENT, CREATIVE)*.

Additional: Female, approx 16 years old.

This is definitely drawn by someone particularly intelligent. This looks like the drawing of someone who wants to be there on the beach right now. I'd say they have a lot of pressure on them at the moment – particularly from their family. I think this is probably unnecessary stress, judging from how the artist has really let themselves immerse and escape for a moment in the drawing process – the occasionally heavier lines bring them back to reality where their personality often has them trying to please everyone without having enough time for themselves. My impressions from the artist and the drawing were that people don't realize how grown up she has become and may not give her the freedom, it appears, she is looking for at the moment. Obviously, she is very creative and a bit of an idealist – beautiful beach, palm trees. Her personality type is such that people often come to her about their problems or council, and I imagine, whilst she likes being this person she really just wants to be given more time to herself.

Example 2 :: Baaaa-Baaaa!!!

Pressure: Heavy *(NATURAL DRIVE & ENERGY, PASSIONATE)*.

Lines: Hard, Sharp.

Position: Centred and towards right *(ORGANISED, EXTROVERT)*.

Picture: Sheep *(WARM, PROTECTIVE, SENSITIVE)* facing right *(ACTIVE, INDEPENDENT FROM FAMILY)*, four legs, smile *(FRIENDLY, SENSE OF HUMOUR)*, medium ears *(GOOD LISTENER)*, fairly sheepy coat *(ENJOYS LIFE, HEALTHY)*, sun *(SUNNY DISPOSITION)*, birds & flowers and precision of suns rays *(ANALYTICAL, CAUTIOUS)*.

Additional: Female, approx 25 years old.

Let's start by looking at the pressure of the drawing. What I'm getting from this, is someone with a lot of drive and natural energy. This is reinforced by the sheep facing right, suggesting you are a very active person. I'd say you are enjoying your freedom right now and although you have a few questions, relating to where exactly your life is going, you feel particularly free at the moment and are exercising your independence or freedom from your family. The positioning of the sheep and the extra little details suggests you are someone to whom details matter – the devil is in the details – perhaps this leads you to over analyze situations and to your being a bit cautious of people or situations; an idea reinforced by the sheep, which although is generally portrayed as a happy, carefree animal, it is also a highly cautious animal.

Generally, someone who draws animals is either an animal lover or a sensitive and protective person – often with family and close friends. Optimistic and happy...they probably have a good sense of humour too.

Example 3 :: Tree!

Pressure: Medium *(WELL-BALANCED, CONFIDENT)*.

Lines: Straight with curves.

Position: Centred, using complete space, orientated vertically *(AMBITIOUS, REACHING UP – CAN PROBABLY HANDLE CONFINED SPACES)*.

Picture: Winter Tree (no leaves) – *(HONEST AND OPEN),* branches reaching out *(DESIRE TO EXPAND HORIZONS),* slightly willow tree'ish *(PROTECTIVE OF LOVED ONES)* wide base *(STRONG SENSE OF FAMILY, GOOD CHILDHOOD),* ground present, knot hole present halfway up tree *(TROUBLE OR TRAUMATIC EXPERIENCE AROUND THE AGE OF 15),* sun *(SUNNY DISPOSITION).*

Additional: Male, approx 27 years old.

This is a particularly interesting tree. The pressure, how much force the artist has used to draw the tree, is fairly medium, indicating someone well-balanced and confident and outgoing. The style of tree suggests someone who is open and honest and I suspect their friends would come to them for an honest answer and truthful perspective on something, and that they are probably somewhat of a confident for someone. The willow look to the tree can signify depression, but here I think it shows a strong protective nature towards their friends and family. You are friendly and enjoy having a good time often, you may be the life of the party but I feel you're very introspective and have a small circle of friends you really feel like family with. You have a good strong family background, a fun and cared for childhood...well it had its ups and downs...did you have a particularly traumatic experience halfway through your life, probably at 15/16? Or something that has dramatically affected your life? Does this make sense? The outstretched branches are like arms reaching out to make connections in both social and business situations and they also symbolize growth and the aspiration to reach new levels and horizons.

Example 4 :: The Peeping Sun

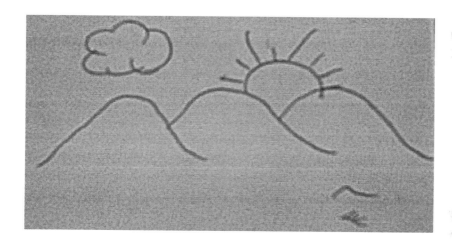

I'm not sure why I picked up this one but I thought it would be nice to talk about some key points using this as an example. I actually cannot remember much about the artist.

The way I would go about reading this would be: The cloud and the sun are particularly interesting. Depending on how I read the person, the sun could have been a sign of an extroverted and optimistic person, who, despite being very ambitious is kind of humble and down to earth in such a way that although they have high ambitions they are aware they need to work hard to achieve them. (I get this from the sun peeking/hiding behind the mountains.) I would say that they've overcome many obstacles in the past, but unfortunately they feel like one is approaching them or perhaps they're even dealing with one now, which is kind of overshadowing their thoughts of late. (Represented by the cloud looming overhead.)

Another direction I could take this is — "I get from the even firm pressure that you're a very applied and hard working person. At the moment you have some troubles looming or overshadowing you...perhaps at work or at home...but it's something that's always on your mind. I'd imagine you would really like to get away from it all right now and take a break. The good news is, you are a strong person and you're ambitious, outgoing and have a lot of natural drive, and this is what will get you over this obstacle. Although you are quite a reserved person, now would be a good time to really let everyone know you are confident and strong."

Example 5 :: BLUB – BLUB – BLURB

Here is a great example of how much flexibility you have with doodle readings, and how it only takes small observations to make a reading.

In this drawing, look at the how the bulk of the drawing is left of centre but the drawing itself is literally reaching out and 'venturing' into the right. A great topic here: **(Essentially the subject is moving from left position personality characteristics to right position personality characteristics**). E.g., perhaps they used to dwell a lot on the past and now they would like to put the past behind them and think more about the future.

In this reading I talked about how it indicated someone who lives more for the moment, but who is often held back by, or quite reflective about the past. I then talked about how the octopus was reaching out to the right, symbolising a search for new social connections or a desire to change and start making steps towards the future and develop plans. They are looking or heading in this direction but still find it hard to change, or don't wish to leave or lose their spontaneous side.

What other things could you say about this drawing? Creative, Artistic, Individual, Unique, Love of Octopi.

Look at the ocean, the waves – maybe the person is feeling pushed or forced by problems or situational circumstances to move towards the right position characteristics, and feel like they are going against their natural flow. Perhaps there is another driving force behind this change?

The Doodle Reading Game

There's a chance you may have already seen me demonstrate this little game; a game I have become quite good at, even if I say so myself. And you can too. It's perfect to practice your people and doodle reading skills, after dinner, or at Christmas or as a party trick... or even on stage!

Give between 3 – 5 people a piece of paper or index card and then have them draw or doodle something on it... but be sure to tell them not to show it to yourself or anyone else. When everyone is finished, have them hand the papers to one person whose job it will be to mix up the pieces of paper so that no-one knows to whom each piece of paper belongs.

Pick one of the pieces of paper at random and tell the artists not to give anything away because you are going to try and tell who drew each one.

Begin by giving your interpretation of the doodle and then using the facts you discover from the doodle and your own knowledge and intuitive impressions of each artist, try and hand the doodles back to the correct person. Sounds simple...well after a little bit of practice it soon will be ;)

The Meaning of Colours and Numbers

Colours

The role colour plays in our lives is easily understated. From an early age we develop preferences for colour – when we begin to establish common ground with people at a young age, and in a foreign language we are often drawn to asking, "What is your favourite colour?". Colour can change our perception, our emotions and attitudes towards something.

Food served on a blue plate suppresses the appetite. Blue is often a sad colour, but also calming. Blue has become quite a 'techy' computer orientated colour. It's also chosen by romantically happy and passionate people.

Red is seen as a warning, danger...it's also sexual and passionate. It's an exciting, adventurous colour. Studies have shown that teams wearing red often have the advantage in competitive events. To the Chinese it's the colour of good luck and hope; you'll often see red ribbons wrapped around Chinese coins to bring good blessings and the prospects of wealth.

White in China is the colour of mourning...not black as we are accustomed to the in West. Pure. Innocent. It's a clean surgical colour. It's also the colour of a blank page. Boring. Uninspired. Waiting. However a particularly creative person may be waiting to fill a white space with colour and art...it holds the promise of something greater.

Green is a natural, calm colour. It's the colour of life, gaia. It's also associated in the Western world with money, the dollar. And the colour of greed is green.

Yellow, although a warm, inspiring colour is also associated with cowardliness, "that yellow-bellied son of a..."

Orange is a creative, warm, inspiring colour. It is a colour we love to see ignite the sky at night. It's also a bright confident colour. Although in America the colour orange may be associated with jumps suit and prisons. It is probably my favourite colour.

Black gets a lot of bad rap and is occasionally nervous and overworked. But it's also sleek and stealthy.

Numbers

Perhaps some of you have seen the TV series "Touch" starring Keifer Sutherland and are familiar with the concept of universal mathematics and of a connection between all of us. Others may also be familiar with Chinese Numerology. "Touch" explored the idea that numbers and maths play a significant part in the way the universe communicates with us and how our future and actions are mapped out and related. This is an idea explored long ago, according to legend, by the Chinese who mapped out the significance of numbers on the back of a tortoise shell. Whether you subscribe to this or not, I have found the exploration of numerology and the appearance of numbers in doodles to be fruitful and worthy of consideration. For instance; the number of flowers and petals (seem to correlate with family size.) But also, you may have seen numbers appear in other ways. Here is a quick run down of the two sides to their meanings.

The number 1 represents creativity, power, success, happiness and prosperity. The other side warns of the power of others over you.

The number 2 represents co-operation, friendship, diplomacy and music. The other side represents restlessness, unsettled conditions and change.

The number 3 represents ambition, religion, authority and health. The other side represents the law, rules and dissatisfaction.

The number 4 represents science, building, mathematics and justice. The other side means rebellion, false dreams and lies.

The number 5 represents adventure, travel, movement and perfection. The other side represents nervousness, guilt and trouble.

The number 6 represents family, personality, love, sex, the arts and magnetism. The other side means lust, anger, debt and wily business deals.

The number 7 represents mysticism, knowledge, study and entertainment. The other side represents folly, misguidance and caution.

The number 8 represents money, business, land and a connection with Earth. The other side means worry and melancholy.

The number 9 represents completion and rebirth, force, energy and power. The other side is about fire, injury and accidents.

The Left Brain - Right Brain

"The intuitive mind is a sacred gift, and the rational mind a faithful servant.
We have created a society that honors the servant but has forgotten the gift."
- - Albert Einstein

The Left Brain / Right Brain has been / is being thrown into general awareness by modern day neurophysiology. The brain is divided into two hemispheres, each of which has its own 'skills'.

The Left Brain is the side of the brain that has been cultivated by modern day living and schooling. It's analytical, goal driven, focused. It understands and handles tools. It's the masculine brain – controlling, it reasons and analyzes. It houses our language centre.

The Right Brain´s hemisphere is becoming dominated by the left. The left actually restricts access to the right in normal waking consciousness. You need to pass through filters and checks to be allowed even close to it. The Right Brain is the feminine, receptive, creative and intuitive side of the brain. It's linked to compassion, empathy and love. It makes connections with the world and with others. It keeps us in contact with the subconscious and the spirit world. Its language is in metaphor, emotions, symbols and the interpretation of archetypes.

There are ways to access and bring the right hemisphere into play. It's the hemisphere and style of thinking I try and use when I interpret doodles. The Right Brain understands these.

We can bring out our intuitive, emotional, creative Right Brain in a few ways. Some of the techniques I use are stemmed in shamanic rituals and traditions.

One of the key techniques I use is Visualization. In social situations this may be as simple as seeing the invisible connections between those I am with and talking to and making that visual connection between the people.

When I have time and wish to tap into my Right Brain, I begin by taking deep breaths — timing each inhalation and exhalation to 3-4 beats of my heart. After a few of these I close my eyes and imagine a blank canvas screen in my mind. On this canvas I visualize and project the colour RED — it may be splashes of paint or the vivid drawing of a red apple. I hold this in my mind. If you can't hold the colour for long that's OK. Keep at it. This will then morph or become dominated by the colour ORANGE: Perhaps a sun, or an orchard of orange trees. Then I see the colour YELLOW like a big bright burning SUN. Then I look down to the luscious GREEN grass on which the sun is shining. Focusing vividly on that one blade of grass, there is a small reflective dew drop trapped on it. Looking into this dew drop I see a vast BLUE ocean of rolling waves beneath a light blue sky. Across the sea comes a VIOLET coloured boat with a large WHITE sail.

By this time I have changed my brainwave patterns and shifted into a more receptive and intuitive gear...this technique is also wonderful when you are experiencing insomnia and need to sleep...and it'll allow you to drift off into the dream state; which itself is a product of the increased receptiveness and openness of the Right Brain.

Doodling Is Good

To start concluding I want to begin by telling you all this: Doodling is Good.

Even in places where it is often frowned upon: for instance in board-rooms, class-rooms, at work and in meetings. In fact, doodling in these situations appears to actually be reeeallly good.

• Doodlers, in studies carried out on the retention of information during a mundane phone call scored 29% better memory retention than the non-doodling test subjects.

• It engages multiple modalities. These are pathways by which we receive information: Visually – Auditory (sound) – Kinesthetic (physical manipulation and exploration). When we engage multiple modalities, we have been shown to learn more and absorb more information. Adding the kinesthetic doodle to the board-room environment actually seems to improve our focus and input in these situations. Doodling seems to bring out creativity and serves as a conduit for ideas.

• In fact introducing doodling, drawing and graphic mind-maps produced through group participation has resulted in a near unrivaled level of co-operation in the workspace alongside a more efficient, innovative Right-Brained approach to problem solving.

So welcome doodling and doodlers, and start incorporating the doodle into your life.

Zen and the Art of Doodling

There is something precious and beautiful in immersing yourself in something.

Let's take a moment to explore a practice that:

- Helps to relax and unwind.

- De-stress.

- Sharpen our focus.

- Allow our brain to reset.

- Decrease our heart rate and blood pressure.

- Promote creativity.

- Stimulate mental function and bring mental clarity.

- ... all whilst creating something beautiful.

In fact, these are also many of the benefits of meditating, but without needing to close your eyes and sit still for long periods of time.

The creation of zentangles, pieces of abstract art made on a small square of paper using unstructured, unplanned, repetitive patterns, allows us to do that. They are very simple to get started on and can take you away from your stresses for anywhere between 15 minutes to 1 hour. There is no artistic talent required and whilst creating some of your own mini masterpieces, you'll find yourself easily relaxing and unwinding, as you focus and immerse yourself in every pen stroke.

To get started, take a look at this little quick-start guide.

1) Find a decent gel black pen or pencil and sharpener.

2) Cut out a nice square of paper about 4" x 4", just to begin with.

3) Load up YouTube with some meditation music, if you haven't already got some. Just search for MEDITATION MUSIC.

4) Divide the square into individual sections, however naturally feels right to you. These are called strings in zendoodle language. Check out this example.

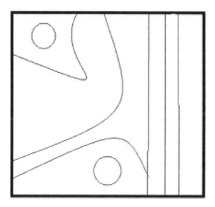

5) Fill in one section with a repetitive pattern. Do not spend too much time worrying about how you might do this, just go with the flow. Later on you can practise with more complex patterns – there will be more information on that towards the end. Then fill in another section with a different pattern. The images above and below were made on a paint program so they are very limited and serve only as quick visual examples.

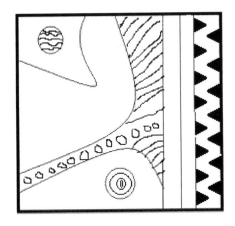

6) Add colour and shading as you wish.

And sit back and admire your artwork.

Patterns

Picking up a cheap book on Zentangles or Zendoodles will provide you with a wealth of patterns and shapes to incorporate in your zendoodling. A Google and YouTube search of phrases like "zentangles" and "zentangle patterns" will provide you with many samples and videos which show the creation of slightly more advanced zendoodles.

Don't forget to be aware of all the patterns around you on clothes, brickwork, trees, honeycombs, leaves, water, animal stripes ... let the world around you inspire your patterns as much as those you find in books and online.

Remember, focus on one stroke at a time and anything is possible.

Exploring Symbolism in Everyday Life

In my dreams, I often drift back thousands of years to when we were all sitting around the first fires, where we watch the flickering of the flames twist, morph – throwing and bouncing shadows around the cave walls.

We bang together rocks and logs and create the first music. We listen to the rhythm of water droplets as they fall from the ceiling and gather in pools... the distant rumbling of thunder, the soft heartbeat of another resting close by, everything is an inspiration for us.

Around these first fires the first forms of dance and expression come into being. We tell stories, re-enact hunts and share our dreams.

A wizened hand, skin cracked and tough, reaches into the ashes of a dying fire, raking together the glowing embers to keep the first source of heat and light alive, and in doing so discovers that marks can be created with the blackened wood. Soon comes drawings, crude, yes, but full of meaning, depicting the world around us, the animals that feed us, our great adventures — and ourselves!

The fire flickers. We search for answers. Our dreams serve as oracles and a connection with a world we couldn't see or touch. The fire provides us with warmth, and protection... why wouldn't it give us answers too, if we looked at it long enough? If we fed it with twigs, shells, rocks or blood?

Our brain's language is imagery and metaphor. In our dreams guidance and knowledge is imparted through this metaphorical imagery and in the same way it finds the answer and solution to problems in our waking life. It is my belief that it is in much the same manner that the various oracles, tarots, and divination systems work. Our brain finds in them (oracle readings e.g. tarot) pieces of metaphor and imagery that serve as tools to apply and work with problems it may be facing and it's through these and the subconscious processing that we find ourselves understanding an issue more profoundly or previously hidden gateways and pathways are uncovered.

The oldest *known* (read: discovered, surviving) cave art, which is found in Northern Spain goes back an estimated 40,800 years. And it wouldn't be a far stretch to say that probably centuries, millennia before that, man first realized that using the embers from the dying fire or the red mud left over after the rain, he could make marks on the wall. The evolution from making a mark to crudely painting the world around him and the images he saw in his dreams would have come next.

We have some 40,000 years of symbolism innate within us and that we see represented in the world around us. Whether analyzing doodles, drawings, dreams or people we can refer back to this wealth of symbolism, learn from it and notice how it changes and the world is changing with it.

In your path to understanding symbolism I ask you to take a look around you. What do the things in your life symbolize? How about the watch you wear? The flowers in your garden ... and the traditions you follow? Have you ever wondered exactly why holly and ivy are so symbolic of Christmas and winter? How about your favourite animal? — Take a moment now to research the symbolic meanings of your favourite animal. How does it change cross-culturally?

Dreams

Finally I ask you to pay attention to your dreams. They are truly a magical part of us and, I believe, easily the least understood. We spend a third of our life sleeping. In this time we are exploring a different plane of consciousness — our soul taking flight along a different path. The aboriginals say through the dreamworld we have access to everything: the past and the future. You may have noticed that you have a dream memory - previous dream occurences and dreamscapes will be recalled from previous dreams and elaborated upon, revisited or contemplated upon during your dreams. There is sooo much going on that we are not aware of.

I've been recording and working with the messages in my dreams for a number of years now. I make it common practise to record my dreams. Make a written note of anything you remember or that stood out particularly in your dream. As the days, weeks and months go by, look for reoccurring imagery, metaphor and patterns. What might your dreams be telling you? Are they preparing you for events in the future? Sharing moments with loved ones present and passed on?

When recording a dream, I start by giving it a title as if it were a movie. I note the date and then write out as much of the dream as I can remember. I include details of how I felt in the dream and the colours that were there. I then write down how I felt when I woke up, and whether any part my dream could occur in my waking life.

Synchronicities

I've just begun keeping a journal of all the synchronicities and coincidences I experience. I see these synchronicities as a nod and wink from the universe that there is some marvelous poetic act unfolding — sometimes we are given the role of the weaver. Notice how at times we meet someone new and then suddenly begin seeing them everywhere. Perhaps this is a thread given for us to weave and see the connections related with it? What should one do? Should we miss that chance?

Please begin recording your synchronicities and Deja Vu's and perhaps compare those to the imagery from your dreams. There is so much I don't want you to miss.

Let me leave you with this wonderful facebook status update from a prolific dream worker and teacher, Robert Moss:-

> Mark Twain was ruined when he decided to invest all his money in a machine that promised to make printing more accurate. He failed to notice that he could never spell the name of the machine or its inventor correctly - which might have warned him that something was badly off. A cautionary tale of how we want to pay attention to what may be showing through our slips. - - Robert Moss (www.mossdreams.com)